My head bowed:
A chapbook on depression, anxiety, and faith

Wendelyn Vega

My Head Bowed: A Chapbook on Depression, Anxiety, and Faith © 2018 Wendelyn Vega

All Rights Reserved. No part of this publication may be reproduced, stored in a retrieval system, or transmitted, in any form or in any means — by electronic, mechanical, photocopying, recording or otherwise — without prior written permission except in the case of brief quotations embodied in critical articles or reviews.

Cover photo by Pok Rie from Pexels.com

Cover Design by Wendelyn Vega

ISBN Number

First Edition: January 2018

10 9 8 7 6 5 4 3 2 1

Table of Contents

Oh my trembling faith............................5
I can't put it back together 6
Don't know where to start........................7
So what 8
This is broken 9
Silent. 10
Lovely 11
I am torn........................... 13
Nautilus 14
My eyelids are heavy 16
Float 17
I can't do it 18
A prayer 19
i, the thief, confess............................. 20
I have died 22
Silence 23
Matthew Seven 24
Me........................... 26
Who are you? 27
For Elizabeth: 29

To my parents, who always believed in me. To all others on this journey. And all glory to God.

Oh my trembling faith,
So frail and swiftly broken.
Will Your hands reach me?

I can't put it back together

I can't put it back together.
All broken up, bound, tied,
And pinned, but
I can't put it back together.
Still beats... sort of.
Still loves... sort of.
Still hurts... sort of.
But I can't put it back together.
I wait and I stay and I beg and I plead
but it's all in my head so it's not what I need but
I can't put it back together.
Silent... silent... lifeless... and
I can't put it back together.

Special

Don't know where to start.
Living with a broken heart.
Everything I do is wrong,
Feeling like I don't belong.
Can't get my point across.
Never a gain, always a loss.
Feeling like a nobody,
Just can't
seem to see
What's supposed to be
Special
About me?

So what

So what if I impale myself
With words that burn
Like acid rain?
So what if I am cruel
Although I cannot bear the pain?
And so my heart is cold and grey,
So what, my walls are thin.
Emotions slicing lacerations,
Piercing through my clammy skin.
And so I only bruise myself
With nightmares that I keep.
So what if I am cold and grey;
My problems don't run deep.

This is broken

This is broken.
Hopeless tears,
scalding wounded
patchwork heart.
In all things,
blank, empty,
stagnant questions;
proof-less dreams;
Love believes.
This is waiting.
silent wailing,
torrents burning
fragile armor.
Through all things,
moaning caverns,
icy, trying loneliness,
Love endures.

Silent

Silent.
Louder than anything.
Louder than pain, louder than screams,
Louder than ripping apart at the seams.
Louder than sobs, louder than tears,
Louder than anger that seeps through the years.
Weary.
Colder than anything.
Colder than hatred, colder than snow,
Colder than hurts that can cause you to grow.
Colder than rain, colder than wind,
Colder than bitterness at a fight's end.
Silent.
Weary.
Rest.
"My tornado is resting."

Lovely

Am I lovely?
I want to know.
Am I captivating
Wherever I go?
I put on my makeup;
I straighten my smile.
I try to loose weight,
I improve on my style.
Do you see beauty
When you look at me?
Do you think I'm special,
As good as can be?
I try to be better,
Demure and polite.
Coy and alluring,
Doing everything right.
But sometimes I fail,
I don't like what I see.
When I look in the mirror,
What I look at is me.
I'm not desirable,
And I'm not good.
I want to be perfect,
But I don't think I could.
Am I lovely?

Tell me the truth now.
I'll try to do better
If you'll tell me how.
I want to be wanted;
I need to be me.
I am a woman,
And I'm human, you see.

I am torn

I am torn.
I am severed apart.
Finished, worn,
Yet eager to start.
I dare not dream,
But my hope will not go.
As shy as I seem,
I'm longing to show
My spirit and smile,
My love and my mind.
But is it worthwhile
To be one of a kind?
Here in a box
Built around me,
I reach the locks
But won't use the key.
I see joy drape
from this horrible shelf.
But how shall I escape
What I built for myself?

Nautilus

I have failed.
How many years have I been
Curled into a shell
Protecting my heart from itself?
I can't get in.
I can't get out.
My shadow has allies;
My fire fuels itself;
My soul takes the bruises.
I still feel the pain.
I'm
Dredging the base of the well
For a drop of the water
I'm not sure is there.
I fall
Deeper and deeper into
The mire.
Can my voice
Any longer be heard?
I blink but I can't tell my sight
From the darkness
When did it become so hard to see?
What do I call this
Aching emptiness
Somehow filled with fear?

I can hear it.
They're still outside
And
The shell is cracking.

My eyelids are heavy

My eyelids are heavy
My vision is dim
I'm swift to go off on a tangent or whim
I'm losing my mind!
I'm coming unfurled!
Bored to distraction and dead to the world.

Float

I am sinking far below
the level that I wished.
Far beyond survival's chance,
lower than where no one fished.
Gather all the broken strength
so desperately I try,
though I cannot hear my own words,
I open up and cry:
"Waves above my head do rush,
but I have not drowned.
Though the waters lead the tempest,
stormy, angry, 'round and 'round.
Break the chains and loose the shackles,
lift the weighted heavy coat,
fly above the raging waters,
lift me up, God help me float."

I can't do it

I can't do it! My hands are too small
And too soft to reach, I can't touch it at all.
I can't do it, I can't cross this line,
But there is a Hand that is larger than mine.

I can't take it! My heart is too hurt,
And too broken, and hardened, and covered with dirt.
Thorns of resentment do swiftly intwine,
But there is a Heart that is purer than mine.

I can't make it! My will is too weak,
So I don't dare to lift up my head or to speak.
I just cover my eyes and pretend that I'm fine,
But there is a Will that is stronger than mine.

I need help, Lord, my faith is too thin;
sometimes I doubt, disbelieve I can win.
But I know, though sometimes I may ask for a sign,
That there is no God that is greater than mine.

A prayer

Father,
You have placed me here,
In this land of endless pain.
You place me here,
But not alone.
I fight
for You have commanded.
You speak.
I obey.
I draw my sword.

i, the thief, confess...

i, the thief, confess
that i was undeniably wrong.
refusing to see that which i had created,
wrongly, blinding myself to the truth.
that i, this thief, was mistaken.
my choice was bold and blatantly incorrect.
i, as though i stood in another eden
before another tree,
foolish flesh,
plucked myself from Your hand.
again and again and again and again.
i thought that i knew what was to be done,
who i need to be, that i could create myself.
so i drew for myself a design of myself that
i could not create apart from You,
and showed this self to the world.
not the one You created,
but a marred, twisted copy.
i, the thief confess
that i, even reluctantly, relinquish my self-wrought
right
to rule my rueful wretchedness.
i implore You, whom i have failed,
forgive my audacity, the foolishness,
my confidence.

i humbly face myself, erase myself,
and place myself in Your Hands.

I have died

I have died.
Once burning alive,
And not just my heart,
Encased in white stone.
Once like a forest,
now brittle and dry.
Ashes remain where
the seed had once grown.
Revive me
So that I may
Die again.
I have died.
Because I have lived
Trying to be whole
with only one part.
Because words that did breathe
Are now empty and stale,
The work once begun
Must reverse and restart.
Revive me
So that I may
die with You.
I am crucified with Christ: nevertheless I live; yet not I, but
Christ liveth in me: and the life which I now live in the flesh I

live by the faith of the Son of God, who loved me, and gave himself for me.

Silence

Silence is my only word.
All the others You have heard.
Every groan and all complaints
Poured on you without restraints.
I have nothing new to say,
But maybe it is best this way.
Without my words' consistent drum
Your words, transcending mine, may come.
Lord, grace this humble, hurting youth.
Please fill me with your hope and truth.
Include me in your blessed host
Who in silence learned the most.

Matthew Seven

Once.
Twice.
Three times you seek
Till your thoughts become heavy;
Your knees become weak.
Once.
Twice.
Three times you look,
But the path you must take
Seems the path that you took.
Once.
Twice.
Three times you ask
If you haven't been given
Too daunting a task.
You wait and you look
And you ask and you seek,
And you know that your strength
Has long since reached its peak.
Your heart is on fire and
Your eyes start to burn.
And you wonder how much
You could still have to learn,
But
Your answer is close

If you'd only just turn
And knock
Once.
Twice…

Keep on asking, and you will receive what you ask for. Keep on seeking, and you will find. Keep on knocking, and the door will be opened to you. For everyone who asks, receives. Everyone who seeks, finds. And to everyone who knocks, the door will be opened.

Me

This is me.
This.
Bitter, shredded, poison-ridden soul.
A blind and messy being,
One empty, shapeless void.
This is me.
And was mine.
Mine.
Lonely, icy, heartache;
Silly, foolish, aimless desires.
Hopeless, hopeless, hopeless
Hopeless.
Mine.
This is me.
This is mine.
This was mine.
But...
for..
You.

Who are you?

Who are you?
Your power,
and glory
sovereignty and majesty,
are expounded upon
Time.
After time.
After.
Time.
I know You are not to be
trifled with.
And yet...
I call you "Father".
You dote upon me
as a child beloved.
Breathtaking sunrises crowned
with watery jewels.
Sunsets of silk and gold,
Your gifts to me.
But then...
You
abide no sin.
Evil is vanquished and
wickedness punished;
You are all just and wise.

Perfect Judge.
But still...
With love You pardon me.
Your blood has saved me.
When I am attacked,
You hold me
in Your arms
And
I am safe
And free.
Who are you really, then,
Almighty Father, Judge and Savior, to me?

For Elizabeth:

The future was past.
Left behind plastic film,
Stolen moments of hope
And dreams unfulfilled.
Captured.
Marked in memoriam
By rough red ribbon
Dividing page from page.
The future was passed.
The page turned
And said
Don't be afraid.

***

A Note from the Author

Dear Reader,

    Thank you for reading this chapbook! Each poem is a window into a moment in my experience with depression and anxiety and an attempt to reconcile that experience with my faith.

    I hope the poetry here and the sentiments expressed in them help you, either by letting you know that you aren't alone or by helping you understand the heart of a loved one a bit better. I wish you the best!

Sincerely,

Wendelyn Vega

www.ingramcontent.com/pod-product-compliance
Lightning Source LLC
Chambersburg PA
CBHW060346080526
44583CB00014B/1076